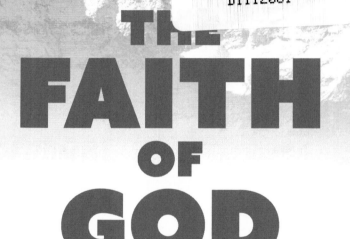

Introduction to

# THE
# FAITH
## OF
# GOD

# Andrew Wommack

Published in partnership between Andrew Wommack Ministries and Harrison House Publishers.

Woodland Park, CO 80862 - Shippensburg, PA 17257

ISBN 13 TP: 978-1-6675-0249-6

ISBN 13 eBook: 978-1-6675-0250-2

For Worldwide Distribution, Printed in the USA

1 2 3 4 5 6 / 25 24 23 22

# Contents

# Permanent Faith

All believers recognize the importance of faith. Faith is critical to our relationship with the Lord. Without faith, it's impossible to please Him (Heb. 11:6). All things are possible to him who believes (Mark 9:23). You were saved by grace through faith (Eph. 2:8).

The question isn't, "Do we need faith?" The question is, "Do we *have* faith?" and if so, "How much do we have?" "Is it enough?"

*Here's the answer.*

**You have the same quality and quantity of faith that Jesus had. It's not your faith in Him but His faith in you. It came as a part of your salvation.**

Those are astounding statements that most Christians don't embrace. The average Christian believes faith works, but they just don't think they have much of it. They are constantly trying to increase their faith.

Jesus' disciples thought this same way. They asked the Lord to increase their faith in Luke 17:5. Jesus answered their request with a parable.

The average Christian believes faith works, but they just don't think they have much of it.

*"And the Lord said, If ye had faith as a grain of mustard seed, ye might say unto this sycamine tree, Be thou plucked up by the root, and be thou planted in the sea; and it should obey you. But which of you, having a servant plowing or feeding cattle, will say unto him by and by, when he is come from the field, Go and sit down to meat? And will not rather say unto him, Make ready wherewith I may sup, and gird thyself, and serve me, till I have eaten and drunken; and afterward thou shalt eat and drink? Doth he thank that servant because he did the things that were commanded him? I trow not. So likewise ye, when ye shall have done all those things which are commanded you, say, We are unprofitable servants: we have done that which was our duty to do."*

(Luke 17:6–10)

Let's look a little closer at Jesus' response. First, He said they didn't need a lot of faith. Faith is so powerful that a tiny amount, like a grain of mustard seed, is enough to pluck up a tree and cast it into the sea. They didn't need more faith; they just needed to use what they had.

Secondly, a master doesn't think he needs to give his servant a break because he's been working all day. No! He expects him to fulfill his duties before he rests. Likewise, faith is a servant that is supposed to be used. Faith isn't rare so that we only use it on special occasions and then let it rest. It's the normal Christian walk (2 Cor. 5:7). The just live by faith (Gal. 3:11); they don't vacation there.

The truth is that every believer already has faith. We were born again by the faith **of** Jesus, not just faith **in** Jesus. We were so destitute that we couldn't even believe the good news of what Jesus did for us without God giving us His faith.

Ephesians 2:8 says, "*For by grace are ye saved through faith; and that not of yourselves: it is the gift of God.*" It's true that our salvation is a gift of God. We can't save ourselves. Eternal life is a gift from God through faith in Christ (Rom. 6:23; 10:9). But it's also true that the faith it takes to receive salvation is a gift from God, too. Think about it. Human faith is based on our five senses: what we see, taste, hear, smell, and feel. Human faith can't believe anything that isn't tangible.

I've heard preachers say it's faith to fly in a plane when you don't know the pilot or how avionics work.

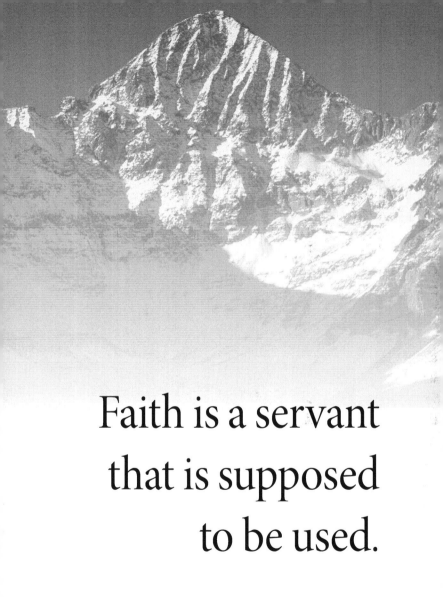

Faith is a servant
that is supposed
to be used.

Human faith can't believe anything that isn't tangible.

It's faith to sit in a chair you've not sat in before. But these are examples of human faith, which everyone has. You have reason to trust a commercial flight. The airline industry is regulated, and there would be severe penalties if they weren't safe. Before you sit in a chair, you look to see if it is solid. If a four-legged chair only had three legs and was leaning, you wouldn't sit in it with a faith that was based on sight.

But when it comes to salvation, you are believing in things that can't be seen or felt. You believe in a God that you've never seen, and you believe that sins you've never seen will be forgiven. You have to believe Jesus forgave and cleansed you. You can't do that with just human faith. Where did that faith come from?

Romans 10:17 says,

*"So then faith cometh by hearing, and hearing by the word of God."*

First Peter 1:23 says,

*"Being born again, not of corruptible seed, but of incorruptible, by the word of God, which liveth and abideth for ever."*

You can't be born again without the Lord imparting faith to you through His Word. He had to impart a supernatural faith to us so we could believe for things we can't see; and that faith doesn't leave or dissipate just because we get saved. The gifts and callings of God are without repentance (Rom. 11:29). God's gift of faith is permanent.

You can't be born again without the Lord imparting faith to you through His Word.

# The Measure of Faith

God's faith is not limited to things that can be seen. In creation, the Lord created light three days before He created a source for the light to come from (Gen. 1:3–19). That's what Romans 4:17 is referring to when it says, "*God… who calleth those things which be not as though they were.*"

Look at what the apostle Paul said in Romans 12:3. "*…God hath dealt to every man **the** measure of faith.*"

At salvation, every Christian received **the** measure of faith, not **a** measure of faith. That's significant. There aren't different measures of faith. We were all given **the** same measure.

Imagine that I was serving soup in a cafeteria line. If I only had one measure, such as a ladle, then everyone would receive **the** measure of soup. But if I used a ladle for some a tablespoon for others, and then a teaspoon for someone else, people would get different amounts.

That's the concept many Christians have. They think the Lord gave different amounts of faith to each believer and that someone jiggled His arm as He was dispensing

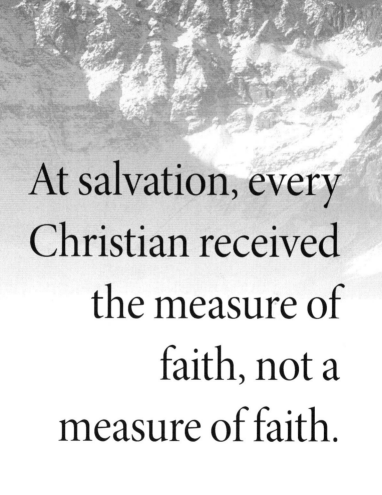

At salvation, every Christian received the measure of faith, not a measure of faith.

theirs. They just don't have much faith. That's not what Romans 12:3 says.

I'm aware that some of the modern translations of Romans 12:3 say, "a measure" instead of "the measure," but that's not correct; and it's verified by other scriptures.

Galatians 2:16 says, "*Knowing that a man is not justified by the works of the law, but by the faith **of** Jesus Christ, even we have believed in Jesus Christ, that we might be justified by the faith **of** Christ, and not by the works of the law: for by the works of the law shall no flesh be justified.*"

Did you see that this verse spoke twice about being justified by the faith **of** Jesus, not just faith **in** Jesus? Then Paul says it again in Galatians 2:20, "*I am crucified with Christ: nevertheless I live; yet not I, but Christ liveth in me: and the life which I now live in the flesh I live by the faith **of** the Son of God, who loved me, and gave himself for me.*"

There it is again. Paul was living by the faith **of** God. Paul didn't just put his human faith in Christ. God gave Paul **the** faith of Christ. Since there is only one measure of faith, then every believer has **the** faith of Christ living in them. We. too, have the same faith Paul had. It's the faith of Jesus.

Since there is only
one measure of
faith, then every
believer has the
faith of Christ
living in them.

Peter said a similar thing in 2 Peter 1:1. "*Simon Peter, a servant and an apostle of Jesus Christ, to them that have obtained like precious faith with us through the righteousness of God and our Saviour Jesus Christ.*"

Peter was writing to people who had received "like precious faith with" him. In this verse, the Greek word *isotimos*, which was translated "like precious," means "of equal value or honor" (*Strong's Concordance*). So, Peter said we have faith that is of equal value and honor to what he had. His faith saw Dorcas raised from the dead (Acts 9:36–42), the lame walk (Acts 3:1–8), and his shadow heal people (Acts 5:15). You have that same measure of faith. If you don't believe that, then tear 2 Peter out of your Bible because it was only written to those with like precious faith.

And notice that Peter said he received that precious faith through the righteousness of God and our Savior, Jesus Christ. His faith didn't come because he was an apostle or lived a holy life. It was the gift of God (Eph. 2:8).

# The God Kind of Faith

In light of all these scriptures that show we have the faith of God, why doesn't every Christian believe this? The number-one reason this isn't commonly understood and believed is because this God kind of faith is in our born-again spirit and not our flesh. In other words, you can't see or feel faith. It's in the unseen realm, and most people walk by sight and not by what God's Word says.

So, by observation, people don't see or feel like they have much faith, and they let what they feel trump what God's Word says. But Philemon 1:6 says **our faith becomes effective by acknowledging what we have, not praying for more faith**. The God kind of faith is present in every true believer. It's just in the unseen spiritual realm. Some people believe that the faith they have might be like God but it's in an immature form that has to be developed. I've heard people say our born-again spirit is complete like a baby is complete. A baby has all the fingers and toes they will ever have, but they have to grow and develop. Likewise, our born-again spirits have faith, but it's in an immature form. But that's not what the Word of God teaches. I have

People don't see or feel like they have much faith, and they let what they feel trump what God's Word says.

dozens of hours of teaching that explain this in much greater detail. My teaching, *Spirit, Soul, and Body* probably deals with that clearer than anything else I could offer. I won't go into all of that in this brief booklet, but let me just use one scripture from 1 John 4:17 to illustrate that our God kind of faith is already complete in our spirits:

> *Herein is our love made perfect, that we may have boldness in the day of judgment: because as he is, so are we in this world.*

That's an amazing revelation that can only be understood in regard to our born-again spirits being like Jesus. Our bodies and souls are awaiting transformation, but our spirits are like Him now. Notice it says, *"...as he is, so are we in this world."* Jesus is complete. He's not growing into perfection. He's perfect now, and so is your born-again spirit and therefore, your faith.

It's our souls (mind, will, and emotions) that are growing in our understanding of faith and how it works. But in our spirits, we have the faith **of** Jesus now. Praise the Lord!

# How to Use Faith

So, the quantity and quality of faith isn't our problem. Faith is a fruit of the Holy Spirit, which every believer has (Gal. 5:22). We have faith, and it's the same faith that Paul, Peter—all the faith giants—and even Jesus had. If that's so, why don't we see that faith work for us?

Right after Peter said he was writing to those with like precious faith with him, he said, *"According as his divine power hath given unto us all things that pertain unto life and godliness, through the knowledge of him that hath called us to glory and virtue:"* (2 Pet. 1:3).

The problem isn't a lack of faith but rather a lack of knowledge about what we have and how to use it. If we don't know we have the faith of Jesus, we won't even attempt to use it. We will just keep believing the lie that what we have isn't enough. What we don't know is killing us. As Hosea said, *"My people are destroyed for lack of knowledge..."* (Hos. 4:6).

There are multitudes of Christians who don't know it's God's will to heal, deliver, and prosper them; and therefore, they don't receive those blessings. It won't

The problem isn't a lack of faith but rather a lack of knowledge about what we have and how to use it.

happen without them first of all acknowledging what is theirs. As Paul told Philemon when he prayed for him, *"...the communication of thy faith may become effectual by the acknowledging of every good thing which is in you in Christ Jesus"* (Philem. 1:6). This faith of Jesus only works for us if we know what we have. The first step is to understand what's ours, and then we have to learn how to use it.

To learn how to use faith, it's important to understand there are laws that govern God's faith. Paul spoke about the "law of faith" (Rom. 3:27). Just as there are laws that govern this physical world, there are laws that govern the spiritual world and the God kind of faith. Take electricity as an example. Electricity has existed since the Lord created the earth. Lightning and static electricity have been with us since the beginning. But man didn't learn how to harness electricity and use it for our benefit until the 1800s. It was our lack of understanding that kept people from using electric lights and all our modern conveniences for thousands of years. And likewise, it's people's lack of knowledge that keeps them from understanding and using this supernatural, God kind of faith. If a person violates the laws governing electricity, it's not the electric company that kills them as punishment. Sure, the electric company generates

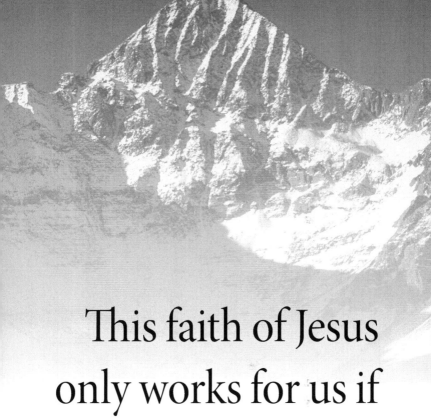

This faith of Jesus
only works for us if
we know what
we have.

the power, but there are laws that govern electricity. If you touch a live wire and are grounded, you will "reap" the results. In a similar way, Christians violate God's laws concerning faith, and it has terminal results. And if someone wants the lights turned on in their house, they don't call the electric company and ask them to turn on the lights. The power company generates the power, but they place it at your command. You have to turn on the switch. They won't do it for you.

# Commanding God's Power

Isaiah 45:11 says, *"Thus saith the Lord, the Holy One of Israel, and his Maker, Ask me of things to come concerning my sons, and concerning the work of my hands command ye me."*

In the same way the electric company has placed their power at your command, so the Lord has placed His power of faith at our command. We have to command His power. This doesn't mean we are the boss and superior to the Lord, so He has to do whatever we command. No. Just as with the lights coming on, we aren't the source. We could put a light bulb in our mouth, and it will never light up; but we have to flip the switch to use the power. It's at our command. Likewise, we are not the source of God's power, but God's power has been placed at our command. If we don't know what we have and learn how to use it, then we will do without seeing the results just as surely as humans went thousands of years without the benefit of electricity.

What are some of the laws that govern the release of God's power?

We are not the source of God's power, but God's power has been placed at our command.

A good example of this is found in Mark 5:25–34, in the story of the woman with the issue of blood.

*"And a certain woman, which had an issue of blood twelve years, And had suffered many things of many physicians, and had spent all that she had, and was nothing bettered, but rather grew worse, When she had heard of Jesus, came in the press behind, and touched his garment. For she said, If I may touch but his clothes, I shall be whole. And straightway the fountain of her blood was dried up; and she felt in her body that she was healed of that plague. And Jesus, immediately knowing in himself that virtue had gone out of him, turned him about in the press, and said, Who touched my clothes? And his disciples said unto him, Thou seest the multitude thronging thee, and sayest thou, Who touched me? And he looked round about to see her that had done this thing. But the woman fearing and trembling, knowing what was done in her, came and fell down before him, and told him all the truth. And he said unto her, Daughter, thy faith hath made thee whole; go in peace, and be whole of thy plague."*

This woman had suffered bleeding for twelve years and spent all of her money trying to find a cure. She finally came to Jesus and was instantly healed. That's awesome, but there are some very important keys to this healing that are often overlooked.

First of all, notice that Jesus didn't know who touched Him (v. 30). Most people believe it was just a rhetorical question on Jesus' part when He said, "Who touched me?" He was God, so surely He knew who touched Him. But remember that Jesus, "...*increased in wisdom and in stature, and in favor with God and man*" (Luke 2:52). Jesus didn't come out of the womb speaking Hebrew or knowing how to walk or feed Himself. He was Lord at His birth (Luke 2:11), but that was in His Spirit. In the flesh, He was a baby with human limitations. He wasn't sinful, but He was limited to a physical body and didn't know all things in His physical mind. I believe He meant exactly what He said: "Who touched me?"

This is very important because most people believe the Lord can do anything He wants to do. When a loved one that we've been praying for dies, I've often heard the question; "Why didn't the Lord heal them? He's God. He could have healed them if He wanted to." That leads those left behind into doubts and bitterness. But that doesn't square with Scripture. When Jesus was in His hometown, the Scripture says, *"And he could there do no mighty work, save that he laid his hands upon a few sick folk, and healed them. And he marvelled because of their unbelief..."* (Mark 6:5–6).

Notice that it says He *couldn't* do mighty works, not that He *wouldn't* do them. And it was because of their unbelief. It wasn't a lack of compassion or power on His part, but their unbelief stopped Jesus from doing what He wanted to do. Just as electricity doesn't flow through rubber the way it flows through copper, so God's power doesn't flow through unbelief the way it flows through faith.

Since this healing power flowed through Jesus to the woman with the issue of blood without Him knowing who touched Him, we can see that healing isn't dispensed on a case-by-case basis. There are just laws that govern healing; and when those laws are used, God's power just flows. Just as surely as electricity flows through copper, God's power flows when the laws of faith are in place.

Just as surely as electricity flows through copper, God's power flows when the laws of faith are in place.

# 4 Laws of Faith

Law #1: Faith comes by hearing God's Word.

Notice that the woman with the issue of blood heard about Jesus (Mark 5:27). That corresponds with "*faith cometh by hearing, and hearing by the word of God*" (Rom. 10:17). One of the laws of faith is that faith is based on knowledge, specifically the knowledge of God's Word. That's what Peter went on to say in 2 Peter 1:4, "*Whereby are given unto us exceeding great and precious promises: that by these ye might be partakers of the divine nature, having escaped the corruption that is in the world through lust.*"

The Word of God gives us the knowledge of God. This woman not only heard about Jesus, which brought her faith, but then she acted on that faith. She got up and did something.

Law #2: Faith without works is dead.

James 2:20 says, "*...faith without works is dead.*" One of the laws that governs faith is that faith has to have corresponding actions. Those who say they believe, but then act contrary to what they say, stop that faith from producing.

If we were together in a building and I told you the building was on fire and we would die if we don't escape, that would cause you to do something if you really believed me. You might panic. You might faint. You might try and put out the fire or run for your life. But if you just sat there doing nothing, that would indicate you didn't really believe me. True faith causes actions. Those who say they believe the Lord but all their actions are contrary to what they say are just deceiving themselves. Faith has to be acted upon. This woman didn't just hear about Jesus, she got up and went to Him.

Law #3: Faith is voice activated.

One of the most neglected laws of faith is failing to use the power that is in our words. This woman said, *"For she said, If I may touch but his clothes, I shall be whole."* **Faith is voice activated.**

Proverbs 18:21 says, *"Death and life are in the power of the tongue: and they that love it shall eat the fruit thereof."* Faith has to be spoken.

I had a man come up to me once, and he said he knew all the healing scriptures, but he just didn't have the power to receive his healing. I quoted Proverbs 18:21 to him and told him he had power right there in

# True faith causes actions.

his mouth. But notice that verse didn't say only life was in the power of the tongue. It said *"death and life"* are in the power of our words. This man had power in his words, but he was only using them to release death. He was verbalizing his doubt not his faith. He was hung by his tongue.

In Mark 11, Jesus cursed a fig tree with His words. He didn't touch the tree or put salt on it. He didn't do anything in the natural. He just spoke that no one would ever eat figs from that tree again. He used His words.

It didn't look any differently in the natural, but immediately the tree died from the roots up. In the morning when Jesus and His disciples walked by that same fig tree, Peter notice that the tree was dried up from the roots. This amazed him, and he called Jesus' attention to it.

Jesus told Peter how this happened, in Mark 11:22–24: *"And Jesus answering saith unto them, Have faith in God. For verily I say unto you, That whosoever shall say unto this mountain, Be thou removed, and be thou cast into the sea; and shall not doubt in his heart, but shall believe that those things which he saith shall come to pass; he shall have whatsoever he saith. Therefore I say unto you,*

*What things soever ye desire, when ye pray, believe that ye receive them, and ye shall have them."*

There are many profound truths that are keys to receiving from God in Jesus' teaching here. I just want to point out that Jesus emphasized speaking faith three times in one verse (Mark 11:23). He said we could have what we say, but most people only say what they have. There is a big difference.

Law #4: Faith can't be mixed with unbelief.

James 1:5–8 says, *"If any of you lack wisdom, let him ask of God, that giveth to all men liberally, and upbraideth not; and it shall be given him. But let him ask in faith, nothing wavering. For he that wavereth is like a wave of the sea driven with the wind and tossed. For let not that man think that he shall receive any thing of the Lord. A double minded man is unstable in all his ways."*

Faith cannot be diluted by unbelief and still accomplish the task. Look at the instance when a father brought his demon-possessed son to Jesus for deliverance.

*"And when they were come to the multitude, there came to him a certain man, kneeling down to him, and saying, Lord, have mercy on my son: for he is unatic, and sore vexed: for ofttimes he falleth into*

Faith cannot
be diluted by
unbelief and still
accomplish
the task.

*the fire, and oft into the water. And I brought him to thy disciples, and they could not cure him. Then Jesus answered and said, O faithless and perverse generation, how long shall I be with you? How long shall I suffer you? Bring him hither to me. And Jesus rebuked the devil; and he departed out of him: and the child was cured from that very hour. Then came the disciples to Jesus apart, and said, Why could not we cast him out? And Jesus said unto them, Because of your unbelief: for verily I say unto you, If ye have faith as a grain of mustard seed, ye shall say unto this mountain, Remove hence to yonder place; and it shall remove; and nothing shall be impossible unto you. Howbeit this kind goeth not out but by prayer and fasting."*

Matthew 17:14–21

Jesus wasn't present at first, and Jesus' disciples were unable to cast the spirit out of the boy on their own. When Jesus came on the scene, He did what His disciples were unable to do, and they asked Him why they couldn't do it (Matt. 17:19). Jesus' answer to His disciples reinforces the point I've been making throughout this whole booklet. He told them, *"...Because of your unbelief..."* (Matt. 17:20).

He didn't tell them it was their *"little faith"* as the NIV has translated it. If "little faith" had been the problem, then the rest of verse 20 would make no sense. The rest of verse 20 goes on to say, *"...If ye have faith as a grain of mustard seed, ye shall say unto this mountain, Remove hence to yonder place; and it shall remove; and nothing shall be impossible unto you."* A mustard seed is the smallest of all herbs (Mark 4:31). Jesus was saying that the smallest amount of faith was enough to cast a mountain into the sea, but unbelief negates or dilutes faith. Even the smallest amount of pure faith is sufficient to accomplish anything. But unbelief insulates us from the power of faith the way rubber insulates us from electricity.

The problem with the disciples wasn't a lack of faith but an abundance of unbelief. Instead of trying to get more faith, we need to focus on getting rid of unbelief so **the** measure of faith can work unhindered.

The next verse, Matthew 17:21, tells us how to get rid of unbelief. (Notice that the NIV didn't even put Matthew 17:21 in their translation.)

*"Howbeit this kind goeth not out but by prayer and fasting."*

Even the smallest amount of pure faith is sufficient to accomplish anything.

The subject of the previous verse was the disciple's unbelief. This verse is saying that the way we get rid of unbelief is through prayer and fasting. Prayer and fasting puts our attention on the spiritual realm and denies our carnal realm, where all our unbelief comes from.

Prayer and fasting puts our attention on the spiritual realm and denies our carnal realm.

# What We Already Have

We already have the faith of Jesus in our born-again spirit. We don't have a faith problem. We have a knowledge problem. There are laws that regulate faith and what and how it will produce. We have to learn these laws in order to make our faith effective.

These truths transformed the way I believe and receive from the Lord. Before I understood this, I spent most of my time begging the Lord to give me what I already had. How is the Lord going to answer a prayer like that?

If I gave you my Bible and you had it in your hand, but then you asked me to give you my Bible, how would I respond? I probably would not know how to respond. You already have what you are asking for. I might just be silent, wondering what your problem is.

That's similar to the way the Lord responds to many Christians' prayers. He's silent. We're asking for things He has already given us, and there is no response.

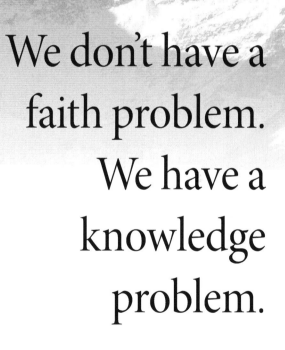

We don't have a faith problem. We have a knowledge problem.

We need to acknowledge what we already have, and start learning how to use it.

I have multiple teaching series that deal with these truths in much more detail. One series is called *The Believer's Authority*. *You've Already Got It*, *The Power of Faith Filled Words*, and *God Wants You Well* are also teachings that cover these topics. The teaching that deals with how to overcome unbelief in the most detail is titled *Hardness of Heart*.

You can receive these teachings in book format, on CD or DVD, or for free on our website. Please call our Helpline 24/7 at (719) 635-1111 or go to awmi.net.

We need to acknowledge what we already have, and start learning how to use it.

# Receive Jesus as Your Savior

Choosing to receive Jesus Christ as your Lord and Savior is the most important decision you'll ever make!

God's Word promises, *"That if thou shalt confess with thy mouth the Lord Jesus, and shalt believe in thine heart that God hath raised him from the dead, thou shalt be saved. For with the heart man believeth unto righteousness; and with the mouth confession is made unto salvation"* (Rom. 10:9–10). *"For whosoever shall call upon the name of the Lord shall be saved"* (Rom. 10:13). By His grace, God has already done everything to provide salvation. Your part is simply to believe and receive.

Pray out loud: "Jesus, I confess that You are my Lord and Savior. I believe in my heart that God raised You from the dead. By faith in Your Word, I receive salvation now. Thank You for saving me."

The very moment you commit your life to Jesus Christ, the truth of His Word instantly comes to pass in your spirit. Now that you're born again, there's a brand-new you!

Please contact us and let us know that you've prayed to receive Jesus as your Savior and to receive some free materials to help you on your new journey. Call our Helpline: **719-635-1111** (available 24 hours a day, seven days a week) to speak to a staff member who is here to help you understand and grow in your new relationship with the Lord.

Welcome to your new life!

# Receive the Holy Spirit

As His child, your loving heavenly Father wants to give you the supernatural power you need to live a new life. *"For every one that asketh receiveth; and he that seeketh findeth; and to him that knocketh it shall be opened…how much more shall your heavenly Father give the Holy Spirit to them that ask him?"* (Luke 11:10–13).

All you have to do is ask, believe, and receive!

Pray this: "Father, I recognize my need for Your power to live a new life. Please fill me with Your Holy Spirit. By faith, I receive it right now. Thank You for baptizing me. Holy Spirit, You are welcome in my life."

Congratulations! Now you're filled with God's supernatural power.

Some syllables from a language you don't recognize will rise up from your heart to your mouth (1 Cor. 14:14). As you speak them out loud by faith, you're releasing God's power from within and building yourself up in the spirit (1 Cor. 14:4). You can do this whenever and wherever you like.

It doesn't really matter whether you felt anything or not when you prayed to receive the Lord and His Spirit. If you believed in your heart that you received, then God's Word promises you did. *"Therefore I say unto you, What things soever ye desire, when ye pray, believe that ye receive them, and ye shall have them"* (Mark 11:24). God always honors His Word—believe it!

Please let us know that you've prayed to be filled with the Holy Spirit and to receive some free materials we have for you. We would like to rejoice with you and help you understand more fully what has taken place in your life. Call our Helpline: **719-635-1111** (available 24 hours a day, seven days a week).

# Call for Prayer

If you need prayer for any reason, you can call our Helpline 24 hours a day, seven days a week at 719-635-1111. A trained prayer minister will answer your call and pray with you.

Every day, we receive testimonies of healings and other miracles from our Helpline, and we are ministering God's nearly-too-good-to-be-true message of the Gospel to more people than ever.

So I encourage you to call today!

# About the Author

ANDREW WOMMACK'S life was forever changed the moment he encountered the supernatural love of God on March 23, 1968. As a renowned Bible teacher and author, Andrew has made it his mission to change the way the world sees God.

Andrew's vision is to go as far and deep with the Gospel as possible. His message goes far through the *Gospel Truth* television program, which is available to nearly half the world's population. The message goes deep through discipleship at Charis Bible College, headquartered in Woodland Park, Colorado. Founded in 1994, Charis has campuses across the United States and around the globe.

Andrew also has an extensive library of teaching materials in print, audio, and video—most of which can be accessed for free from his website: awmi.net.

## CONTACT INFORMATION

Andrew Wommack Ministries Inc.

PO Box 3333

Colorado Springs CO 80934-3333

Email: info@awmi.net

Helpline: 719-635-1111

Helpline available 24/7

Website: www.awmi.net

# Andrew's
# LIVING COMMENTARY BIBLE SOFTWARE

Andrew Wommack's *Living Commentary* Bible study software is a user-friendly, downloadable program. It's like reading the Bible with Andrew at your side, sharing his revelation with you verse by verse.

## Main features:

- Access to Windows, Mac, and web versions
- Andrew Wommack's notes on over 25,000 Scriptures and counting
- 11 Bible versions, 5 commentaries, 3 concordances, and 2 dictionaries
- Maps and charts
- User notes
- Enhanced text selection and copying
- Commentaries and charts
- Scripture-reveal and note-reveal functionalities
- "Living" (i.e., constantly updated)
- Quick navigation
- Robust search capabilities
- Automatic software updates
- Mobile phone and tablet support for web version
- Screen reader support for visually impaired users (Windows version)
- Bonus material

Whether you're new to studying the Bible or a seasoned Bible scholar, you'll gain a deeper revelation of the Word from a grace-and-faith perspective.

Purchase Andrew's *Living Commentary* today at **awmi.net/living**, and grow in the Word with Andrew.

Item code: 8350

**ANDREW WOMMACK** MINISTRIES

## CHARIS
# HEALING
#### UNIVERSITY

The *Charis Healing University* box-set curriculum is made up of extensive teaching and guided application from trusted Bible teachers Andrew Wommack, Barry Bennett, Carlie Terradez, Carrie Pickett, Daniel Amstutz, Duane Sheriff, and Greg Mohr.

*Charis Healing University* contains over 60 hours of teaching spread across **forty-eight online video lessons**, six Q&A panel discussions, and several study resources that have been organized into three different sections:

- **Expect** will build your faith to believe for healing.
- **Experience** will help you know success and receive your healing.
- **Empower** will equip you to minister healing to others with confidence.

The *Charis Healing University* box-set curriculum includes **workbooks** for each section, a **USB** containing audio lessons, and access to our **online course**. The online course gives you access to video lessons and printable PDFs for group study.

Go to **awmi.net/HealingU** or call **719-635-1111**.

Item Code: 6012-U

# Your peace doesn't have to ebb and flow with the tides of circumstance. Build your life on the solid foundation of the Word.

Visit our website for teachings, videos, testimonies, and other resources that will encourage you with truth for any situation and help you learn God's plan for relationships, finances, faith, and more.

*"I was lost deep in the world. . . . I started seeking the truth, and through AWM's resources, I have been set free . . . including receiving miracles of finances when everything seemed impossible. I am at peace with myself. I thank AWM for sharing the truth, which has freed me to understand God."*

— David M.

Be empowered to live the victorious life God intended for you! Visit **awmi.net** to access our library of free resources.

Teaching God's unconditional love and grace.

# CHARIS
## BIBLE COLLEGE

# God has **more** for you.

Are you longing to find your God-given purpose? At Charis Bible College you will establish a firm foundation in the Word of God and receive hands-on ministry experience to **find, follow,** and **fulfill** your purpose.

### Scan the QR code for a free Charis teaching!

**CharisBibleCollege.org**
Admissions@awmcharis.com
(844) 360-9577

Change your life. **Change the *world*.**

**Without *you*, there is no *us*.**

A single drop of water seems insignificant...until it joins with many others to create a river, ocean, or flood. Our partners are like those many drops of water, joining together to flood the earth with the living water of the Gospel.

**Because of our partners, we are able to:**

➢ Teach God's Word through TV, live streams, and conferences broadcast worldwide

➢ Train and equip Charis students around the world to pastor, teach, and disciple

➢ And so much more!

When you partner with Andrew Wommack Ministries, you are reaching lives far beyond your personal sphere. Join us in sharing the Gospel as far and as deep as possible.

Visit **awmi.net/grace** or call **719-635-1111** to become a Grace Partner today!

ANDREW WOMMACK MINISTRIES

# Don't miss
## *The Gospel Truth*
### with Andrew Wommack!

Discover God's unconditional love and grace
and see God in a whole new way!

- ► Hear the Word of God taught
  with simplicity and clarity.

- ► Understand the true Gospel
  message and be set free
  from all kinds of bondages.

- ► Learn how to receive
  your breakthrough.

Go to **awmi.net/video** for local
broadcast times or to watch online.

# AWM Offices

We'd love to hear from you!
Reach out to us at any of our offices near you.

**Andrew Wommack Ministries USA**
Headquarters—Woodland Park, CO
Website: awmi.net
Email: info@awmi.net

**Andrew Wommack Ministries Australia**
Website: awmaust.net.au
Email: info@awmaust.net.au

**Andrew Wommack Ministries Canada**
Website: awmc.ca
Email: info@awmc.ca

**Andrew Wommack Ministries France**
Website: awmi.fr
Email: info@awmi.fr

**Andrew Wommack Ministries Germany**
Website: andrewwommack.de
Email: info@andrewwommack.de

**Andrew Wommack Ministries Hong Kong**
Website: awmi.hk
Email: info@awmi.hk

**Andrew Wommack Ministries Hungary**
Website: awme.hu
Email: hungary@awme.net

**Andrew Wommack Ministries Indonesia**
Website: awmindonesia.net
Email: awmindonesia@gmail.com

**Andrew Wommack Ministries India**
Website: awmindia.net
Email: info@awmindia.net

**Andrew Wommack Ministries Italy**
Website: awme.it
Email: info@awme.it

**Andrew Wommack Ministries Lithuania**
Website: awmi.lt
Email: charis@charis.lt

**Andrew Wommack Ministries Netherlands**
Website: andrewwommack.nl
Email: info.nl@awmcharis.com

**Andrew Wommack Ministries Poland**
Website: awmpolska.com
Email: awmpolska@zyciesozo.com

**Andrew Wommack Ministries Russia**
Website: cbtcrussia.ru
Email: info@cbtcrussia.ru

**Andrew Wommack Ministries South Africa**
Website: awmsa.net
Email: enquiries@awmsa.net

**Andrew Wommack Ministries Uganda**
Website: awmuganda.net
Email: awm.uga@awmcharis.com

**Andrew Wommack Ministries United Kingdom**
Website: awme.net
Email: enquiries@awme.net

**Andrew Wommack Ministries Zimbabwe**
Website: awmzim.net
Email: enquiries@awmzim.net

For a more comprehensive list of all of
our offices, visit **awmi.net/contact-us**.

Connect with us on social media.